AMERICAN INDIAN GAMES

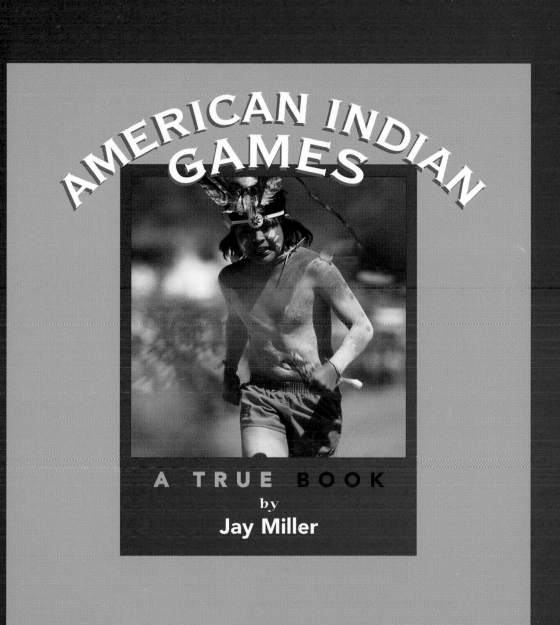

A TRUE BOOK

by

Jay Miller

Children's Press®
A Division of Grolier Publishing

New York   London   Hong Kong   Sydney
Danbury, Connecticut

For help in reading and writing these books, Jay Miller thanks Zachary, Vi, and Rebecca.

Reading Consultant
Linda Cornwell
Learning Resource Consultant
Indiana Department of
Education

Choctaw lacrosse players stretch for the ball.

Library of Congress Cataloging-in-Publication Data

Miller, Jay, 1947-
    American Indian games / by Jay Miller.
        p.   cm. — (A true book)
    Includes bibliographical references and index.
    Summary: Briefly describes some of the toys and games used by various North American Indian cultures to amuse their children and teach lessons about life.
        ISBN 0-561-20136-0 (lib. bdg.)   ISBN 0-516-26092-8 (pbk.)
        1. Indians of North America—Games—Juvenile literature. 2. Indians of North America—Sports—Juvenile literature. [1. Indians of North America—Games. 2. Indians of North America—Social Life and Customs.] I. Title. II. Series.
E98.G2M55 1996
394'.3'08997—dc20   96-13477
                                                                 CIP
                                                                 AC

Contents

Why Play Games?   5

Toys   10

Just for Fun   16

Preparing for Life   20

Part of a Team   25

Special Games   32

New Games   38

American Indian Games Today   40

To Find Out More   44

Important Words   46

Index   47

Meet the Author   48

An Inuit girl enjoys baseball in northern Canada.

Why Play Games?

All over the world, people play games for many reasons. Most people play games because they are fun. But games also can build strong bodies and teach people about sharing and taking turns.

When American Indians play, they remember that games must be played in the right way. Tsimshians, in British Columbia, Canada, tell a story about what happens to noisy children.

Once there was a town where children played games loudly every day. Heaven got angry and sent a feather to float above the town.

The children tried to grab the feather. They stood on each other's shoulders until the chief's son got hold of it and could not let go. Everyone became attached to him

and slowly rose into the air.
They were never seen again.
   Most of all, games helped
American Indians to survive.
Many Indians hunted animals
with bows and arrows. So

Hopi boys shoot arrows through a hoop, almost 90 years ago.

boys all over the Americas practiced using toy bows and arrows to hit a target or a rolling hoop. That took a good eye and careful aim.

Arctic Ocean

Inuit

Inuit

Copper
Eskimos

Inuit

Northwest

Tsimshian

Pacific Ocean

Makah

Plains

Lakota

Cheyenne

Sauk

Iroquois

Oglala

Potawatomi Mohawk

Delaware

Southwest

Hopi Zuni

Atlantic Ocean

Southeast

Choctaw

NORTH AMERICAN
TRIBES

Gulf of Mexico

Caribbean Sea

Toys

American Indian children played games with many kinds of toys.

Many girls had dolls. On the Plains, dolls were made from corn husks, mud, or deerskin. Dolls did not have faces. Lakota girls played house with small tipis.

Toys a Lakota child might have used (top); a carefully made doll—with no face (bottom left); Oglala girls play with tipis in the 1890s (bottom right)

"Jabber" toys could be made in many different ways.

Boys didn't only play with bows and arrows. The jabber, or cup and pin game, kept eyes and hands working together. It was a pointed stick with a string tied to the back end. Attached to the other end of the string were some objects. Players tried to jab the pointed end at the dangling objects until all of them were speared.

In places such as the Northwest, where people traveled by water, children had tiny canoes to learn how to paddle and deal with water flow and dangers.

After it snowed on the Plains, children used sleds made of buffalo ribs tied together. They slid down hills and slopes. Sometimes they ended the trip on frozen streams so they slid far.

A sled made from buffalo ribs

15

Just for Fun

Many games weren't only for children. For fun, everyone learned to make complicated figures using string on their fingers. This game is called cat's cradle, after the name of one of the patterns the string can make. It is played today.

Women were fond of playing with dice, which they

Cat's cradle in the Northwest of Canada (above) and in the Southwest of the United States.

made from fruit pits, bone, wood, or beaver teeth. Each side was painted with differ- ent colors, or decorated with

17

A dice game as it used to be played (above); a Potawatomi bowl and dice (top right); some Cheyenne dice and their carrying bag (bottom right)

dark lines and dots. Each pattern meant a certain number of points. The dice were tossed inside a basket or wooden bowl. If the dice landed with all the same

design up or down, that count-
ed extra.

Men played a guessing game
in which an object was hidden
under one of four moccasins. A
man on the other team had to
guess where a small object,
such as a nut, was hidden.

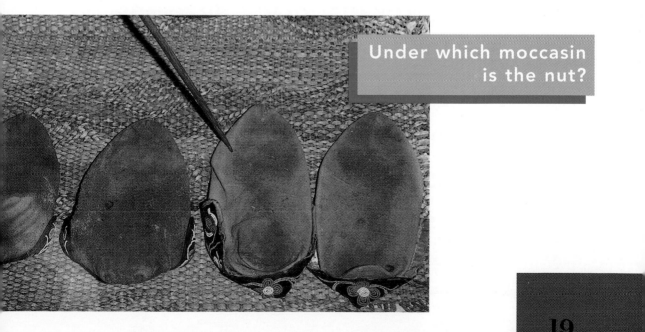

Under which moccasin
is the nut?

Preparing for Life

Games were also part of growing up. Some tribes had baby-talk words that made everyone laugh, or "tongue twisters" that were hard to say. This practice taught people to be careful about what they said and how they said it.

Everywhere, young women

An Inuit teenager learns how to make bannock, a kind of bread.

played house. They did what the women did to take care of their families. They cooked and cleaned. On the Plains, they pretended to butcher buffalo.

In the high, dry lands near the Rockies, they gathered and roasted seeds.

Young men learned to wrestle and play at other sports to grow strong and agile. Teams would pretend to be enemies and fight. They learned to dodge in pretend fights with mud balls or snowballs. They practiced ignoring pain to be brave warriors. In these serious games, they learned to go without food and water and to ignore bruises and

Young Mohawks of today train in a survival school (top). Canoe race on the coast of British Columbia (bottom)

cuts. They wanted to be ready for battles with other tribes or Europeans.

In the Northwest, towns had their warriors race war canoes. Each one had a crew of twelve paddlers. This kept them ready for battle or attack.

Young and old men tested their strength by trying to lift and carry heavy rocks. Often these boulders were decorated with paint or designs chipped into the surface.

During the winter, men or boys played snowsnake. They took turns hurling a ten foot long spear along a groove in the snow or on the ice. The one whose spear went farthest won.

Part of a Team

Some American Indian nations farmed, and so they lived together in large villages. They developed team games.

In the Southwest, men played a kind of kick ball. A round stone was kicked for miles across the desert. The first team of runners to kick their ball over the goal line won the game. Hopi men grew a long, down-curved toenail to protect their big toes from the hard ball.

In the East, tribes created a game called lacrosse or stickball, now played all over the world.

Old Iroquois lacrosse sticks are not that different from those used today.

Each lacrosse player has a racket, a stick with a net on the top end. Iroquois and most other players use only one racket. Tribes of the Southeast, like the Choctaw, use two rackets, one in each hand. Players try to get a three-inch

Choctaw lacrosse players use two rackets.

ball made of wood, or of buck-skin stuffed with hair, into the net and carry it over the goal line. Each side can have only a few members. In big games, there may be hundreds of men.

According to one legend, the first lacrosse game was played by animals against birds. At first, neither side wanted the bat on their team. But the animals finally let him play. They won, because the bat could run and fly. Since then, Choctaw players ask the bat for help. Some will wear something from a bat for luck.

Choctaw players still dress in special ways for luck. Some will play in bare feet or wear a necklace of horsehair because horses run fast. Sometimes, they ask a holy man to pray for them. They believe that it is good to be brave and strong, but not

enough. Players with the strong-
est help from the spirits win.

Long ago, women in many
tribes played shinny, a game like
today's field hockey. Each player
used a stick with a curved end
to hit a ball made of wood, or
stuffed leather, along the
ground.

The Makah in the Northwest
played shinny with two curved
sticks. Each player used one for
hitting the ball and the other
for carrying it to the goal. They
played the game after one of

Shinny being played in Arizona

their leaders had harpooned a whale and brought it to the beach. Everyone feasted and then played shinny using a soft whale bone as the ball.

Today, shinny is still a popular game among American Indians.

Special Games

Some games were played for special reasons. The Delaware played a ball game all summer long to help their crops grow.

Men played against women. The men could only kick the ball, made of leather stuffed with deer hair, and the women could only throw it with their hands. It was like the men were playing soccer and the women were playing football. To win, a team had to take the ball through two goal posts at the east or west end of a long field.

The game was held as a prayer to Corn Mother and the crops. During summer play, the crops grew. In the fall, the Delaware stopped playing because the crops were ready to harvest.

Games were sometimes used to settle arguments. Copper Eskimos of the Canadian Arctic held song duels. Instead of coming to blows, people who were angry with each other sang insulting songs about the other person. A crowd listened, and the person with the most clever song won.

When the Hopi town of Oraibi realized in 1906 that its members were not getting

along, they held a tug of war
to decide who would leave.
The team that got pulled
over a line in the sand had to
leave the town. The people
still live apart.

The Bone Game

When the Spanish came to California, they brought the bone game. Indians learned it. They called this guessing game lahal. They taught it to other tribes. Now everyone in the West plays the bone game.

To play, two teams sit across from each other. A person on one side holds two bone tubes, one plain and the other marked with a black band, in his or her fists.

The other side sings and drums while one of them guesses which hand has the plain bone. The guesser points with his or her finger at one of the fists. The teams use sticks to keep track of the correct number of guesses. When one team wins all twelve sticks, that side wins the game. Then they start another. Other people bet on the outcome of the games.

New Games

From Europeans, Indians
learned to play checkers,
dominos, and chess. They
carved the figures from wood,
bone, stone, and ivory. They
made the playing boards of
leather, wood, and stone.

Indians also learned how to
play card games. They bought

the cards from traders or made them from leather or cedar bark. The Delaware made cards from reeds.

Eskimos carved dominos from ivory. They drilled and darkened the dots by hand.

American Indian Games Today

Like modern youngsters everywhere, American Indian youth play baseball, football, basketball, and track and field sports. Many reservation schools have won regional and state titles in these sports.

Two American Indian junior-
high football teams
in New Mexico (top)
A Zuni Pueblo high-school
cross-country team (bottom)

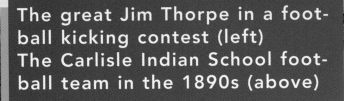

The great Jim Thorpe in a football kicking contest (left)
The Carlisle Indian School football team in the 1890s (above)

The most famous Indian athlete of modern times was Jim Thorpe, a Sauk from Oklahoma. He played football, baseball, and track and field for the Carlisle Indian School in

Pennsylvania. He also won gold medals in the 1912 summer Olympics.

Today, American Indians excel in every modern sport. Yet, they still like to compete in traditional sports such as canoeing, lacrosse, and lahal.

To Find Out More

Here are more places to learn about American Indian games:

Books

Bierhorst, John, ed. **Lightning Inside You, and Other Native American Riddles.** William Morrow and Company, 1993.

Bierhorst, John, ed. **The Sacred Path: Spells, Prayers, and Power Songs of the American Indians.** William Morrow and Company, 1983.

Blood, Charles L. **American Indian Games and Crafts.** Franklin Watts, 1981.

Crum, Robert. **Eagle Drum: On the Powwow Trail with a Young Grass Dancer.** Four Winds Press, 1994.

Organizations

American Indian Athletic Hall of Fame
Haskell Indian Junior
  College
Lawrence, KS 66044

National Museum of the American Indian
Smithsonian Institution
470 L'Enfant Plaza SW
Suite 7103, MRC 934
Washington, DC 20560
Runner@IC.SI.EDU

National Park Service
Office of Public Inquiries
P.O. Box 37127
Washington, DC 20013
(202) 208-4747
http://www.nps.gov

The Southwest Museum
234 Museum Drive
Los Angeles, CA 90065
(213) 221-2164
swmuseum@annex.com

Online Sites

A Guide to the Great Sioux Nation
http://www.state.sd.us/state /executive/tourism/sioux/ sioux.htm

Explore landmarks, legends, art, powwows, and other interesting traditions of the Sioux Nation.

American Indian Resources
http://www.ihs.gov/ 1AmerInd/AI.html

This site contains a complete list of all American Indian tribes, information about them, and links to other sites.

National Museum of the American Indian
http://www.si.edu/organiza/ museums/amerind/

Part of the Smithsonian Institution, this online site is filled with interesting facts and exhibits about Western Hemisphere Indians.

Native American Art Gallery
http://www.info1.com/ NAAG/index.html

Browse the catalog of art and artists and sign up for the gallery's newsletter.

Native Web
http://web.maxwell.syr.edu/ nativeweb/index.html

Discover information about indigenous people all over the world.

Important Words

arrow a stick with feathers on the end and a chipped stone point: shot with a bow, a flexible piece of wood with a strong cord tied to both ends

canoe a small boat made from a hollowed out log or from a wooden frame covered with sheets of bark

culture ideas, actions, and habits that children learn as they grow up in a certain group of people

duel a kind of fight with special rules between two people

moccasin a soft shoe made of leather

spirit an invisible being with special powers

warrior someone trained to fight in battles for his nation

Index

(**Boldface** page numbers indicate illustrations.)

bannock, **21**
baseball, **4,** 40
basketball, 40
bat, 29
bone game, 36–37, **36, 37**
bow and arrow, **7,** 8, **8**
boys, 8, 13
canoes, 14, 23, **23, 43**
cat's cradle, 16, **17**
Cheyenne, **18**
Choctaw, 27, **28,** 29
Corn Mother, 33
cup and pin, **12,** 13
Delaware, 32–33
dice, 16–18, **18**
dolls, 10, **11**
dominos, 39, **39**
Eskimo, 34
football, 40, **41**
girls, 10
hoop target, **8,** 8
Hopi, **8,** 26, 34–35
hunting, 7
Inuit, **4, 21, 35**
jabber. *See* cup and pin

kick ball, 25
lacrosse, **2,** 26–30, **26, 27**
lahal. *See* bone game
Lakota, 10
Makah, 30
men, 19, 22–23, 24, 25–26, 32–33
mocassin game, 19, **19**
Mohawk, **23**
noisy town, 6
Oglala, **11**
playing house, 21–22
Potawatomi, **18**
rock lifting, 24
shinny, 30–31, **31**
sleds, 14, **15**
snowsnake, 24
song duels, 34, **35**
survival school, **23**
Thorpe, Jim, 42–43, **42**
tipis, 10, **11**
tongue twisters, 20
Tsimshian, 6
tug of war, 34–35
warriors, 22, 23
women, 16–19, 21–22, 30–31, 32–33
wrestling, 22
Zuni Pueblo, **41**

Meet the Author

J ay Miller lives in Seattle, visiting nearby reservations, mountains, streams, and the Pacific Ocean. He enjoys eating salmon and pie, hiking in the mountains, and kayaking along the shore as much as he enjoys being a writer, professor, and lecturer. He has taught in colleges in the United States and Canada. He belongs to the Delaware Wolf clan. His family is delightful and very complex. He has also authored *American Indian Families*, *American Indian Festivals*, and *American Indian Foods* for the True Book series.